How To Get Kids To Say YES!

USING THE SECRET FOUR COLOR LANGUAGES TO GET KIDS TO LISTEN

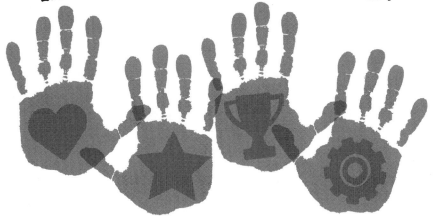

ELLA, LIZ & KEITH SCHREITER

How To Get Kids To Say YES!

© 2016 by Ella, Liz & Keith Schreiter

Published by Fortune Network Publishing
PO Box 890084
Houston, TX 77289 USA

Telephone: +1 (281) 280-9800

Cover Design by Ella Schreiter

ISBN-10: 1-892366-76-2
ISBN-13: 978-1-892366-76-4

CONTENTS

START HERE...

This book is not a psychology case study, or advice on how to raise children. Hey, I am only nine years old.

I am writing this book with my parents. I want to help other parents see and understand their children from a different viewpoint.

Just like adults, kids are all different too. Everything in this world is new to us and we are just finding our way. We test limits and try new things.

We don't have the experience our parents have to help us with our judgments. We aren't old enough yet.

Parents can give us direction and advice more easily if they just recognize our core personality.

This one simple thing makes things so much easier for us. When parents know which one of the color personalities we are, it will be easier and faster to help us to understand. We aren't complicated. We just see, learn, and experiment in our world with one of these unique personalities.

And now from the parents.

Three things you should know about this book.

#1. We are parents, not psychologists.

We just want to understand and help our children.

But like most parents, we don't have time for college courses or weekend seminars on psychology. Children keep us too busy for that.

This book isn't a psychology textbook or course. It is about communicating with our children in a way that helps them to understand us and the world.

So sit back and enjoy this book. It is a fun way to connect with our children and to get along better. It takes some of the frustrations out of being a parent.

No psychologists' jobs will be harmed in the reading of this book.

#2. This is a guide, not a instruction manual.

If you have studied personality profiling before, you know the temperaments: phlegmatic, sanguine, choleric and melancholic. Ugh. That is difficult to remember. Plus, our children don't want to fill out questionnaires and take tests. We are looking for a way to identify how each of our children see the world. Once we know this, we can connect with them, praise them, discipline them and motivate them. (Motivate them?) Yes, children need a little push ... often.

#3. Labeling is dangerous.

We will describe the four basic personality types. As you read this, you will naturally identify with many parts of each personality. One of these personalities might describe your child best. We are looking at the big picture here, so don't worry about the details.

All of the personalities have strengths and weaknesses, ups and down, easy and difficult components. Keep in mind that children are not 100% of one personality. They could have traits that cover two or more personalities.

We don't want to push our child into a corner by labeling them "that type of person." We want them to grow and express themselves freely without trying to conform to some label.

We will look for the most obvious traits and use them as our communication guide. This will help us understand our children's views of us and their world.

Download your FREE Reference Sheet

Use this one page reference sheet as you read *How To Get Kids To Say YES!*

Download it now:

WhatsYourKidsColor.com

THE DREADED UNSOLICITED ADVICE.

Make a simple comment to a friend that we are having an issue with our child. Worse yet, post this on social media.

What happens? The unsolicited advice starts pouring in. Some of the advice is from friends who don't even have children!

All we wanted was some positive affirmation and support from our friends. Instead, we get conflicting advice and the latest theories. Our uninformed friends are telling us what to do. They are not dealing with our child 24 hours a day. They don't know the whole story.

But their advice?

- "This is what you need to do." (I don't know the whole story, but here is the correct solution.)
- "This is what I do." (What I do works for everyone, in every situation.)
- "This is what works for my child." (Your child should be just like my child.)
- "This is what you should do…" (I don't have kids but I saw this television show and they said …)

We hope no one asks us, "So how did it go when you used my awesome advice?" We don't want to hurt their feelings by saying we didn't take their advice.

The reality?

"One size" doesn't fit all.

There is no universal solution that works with every child in every circumstance. Why?

Because children are different. Parents are different. Circumstances are different.

"Why won't you be like child #1?"

Our first-born child arrives. We realize that we need to "figure things out." We try everything. Over time, we find out what works for our firstborn. We know how to keep him happy. We know how to motivate him. We know his needs.

Yes, it took some time but we have it all figured out … until …

The second child arrives.

We think this is going to be easy. We use the same methods to motivate, to keep her happy, and we believe we know what works best for her. And surprise!

Maximum failure.

Why?

She is nothing like our firstborn. In fact, she is the exact opposite!

Our previous experience is useless. Something is different. She is "wired" completely different than our firstborn. We feel like throwing our hands into the air in frustration.

We want answers!

The reality is that our two children were "wired" differently from birth. They will have different viewpoints when observing and reacting to their new world.

Now, we don't have to be a psychologist to see this. We don't need years of training, thick books, and endless lectures to see the obvious. We are living the experience.

The bottom line?

We want to figure out how to make our children's lives better and happier. As an added bonus, if we can communicate with our children better, our lives get easier.

FOUR CHILDREN.

Four completely different personalities.

Same parents.

From infancy, they all seem to engage with the world in different ways.

Child #1 was born to be a nurturer. She practiced with dolls, and loved taking care of her younger siblings. At five years of age, she could feed her younger siblings and couldn't wait to cook the family meals.

Child #2 laughed and loved to be entertained. With a shorter attention span, he needed constant new input to keep his interest. A born extrovert and showman, he was everybody's instant friend.

Child #3 wanted to do everything herself. She insisted on feeding herself and participating in everything her older siblings did.

Child #4 seemed curious about everything in his world. He investigated and carefully experimented with his new surroundings. Naturally introverted, social interaction was not always a high priority. You could see him becoming a scientist.

- Same environment.

- Same parents.

- Four unique personalities.

- Four different ways of viewing and interacting with the world.

This book will be a short, fun and easy manual on how to recognize the four basic personalities in our children. This can help us better understand them by seeing the world through their eyes.

We will learn some basic interaction techniques to connect and communicate with our child in more effective ways.

We like to keep things easy and simple. So, we won't learn any complicated, hard-to-pronounce scientific terms. Instead, we will use four basic colors to describe the personalities. Much easier.

So let's discover the four basic "wirings" or personalities of our children.

WHAT IS THE YELLOW PERSONALITY?

An easy way to recognize and remember the yellow personality? You just need one single word:

"Help."

Not S.O.S. help, but as in, "How can I help others?"

Yellow personalities love to help people. They find satisfaction and fulfillment in helping others to live happier and better lives. The feeling of satisfaction is all the reward they desire.

Look for these dominant characteristics:

- Is more quiet and less outgoing.
- Cares about others.
- Worries about other people's feelings.
- Wants to be part of a team effort.
- Loves fundraising and causes.
- Has a strong desire to protect their family and friends.
- Looks for opportunities to contribute.
- Loves to help other people reach their goals.

- Is not interested in winning personally, but is concerned that other people may feel badly when they lose.

- Is the first to volunteer for projects.

One way to remember the yellow personality is to visualize examples in our minds. Here are some classic examples of yellow personalities:

- Big Bird on Sesame Street. (Perfect example, especially because he is a big yellow bird.)

- Mr. Snuffleupagus on Sesame Street.

- Mr. Rogers from the children's show, Mr. Rogers' Neighborhood.

- Fairy godmothers.

- Elmo. Everyone loves Elmo.

- Homer Simpson's neighbor, Ned Flanders. He is a great example of a happy, friendly, willing-to-help yellow personality.

Charlie Brown.

The comic strip character, Charlie Brown, is the ultimate yellow personality. He always looked to please … everyone. Because he was trying to make everyone happy, he was never able to make a decision to move forward.

Do you remember the Charlie Brown Christmas Special? Charlie Brown offered to buy the Christmas tree. His friends wanted the newer, shinier, more modern Christmas tree. They wanted that indestructible, flashier, imitation Christmas tree.

But not Charlie Brown. He fell in love with a real tree. He fell in love with the saddest, most pathetic, near-death Christmas tree. The tree needed sympathy and love. When Charlie Brown picked up the tree, most of the little tree's brown needles fell to the ground. So sad. Only a yellow personality would pick this needy and helpless tree.

Charlie Brown brings back the Christmas tree. His friends make fun of him. But the teasing doesn't affect Charlie Brown. He won't let anything ruin his Christmas spirit. He says, "I will show them this can work." He does this not to prove his friends wrong, but because he loves that sickly, tiny tree.

Even when Charlie Brown's luck deserts him and the tree doesn't work out, his friend says, "Maybe this tree just needs a little love."

Charlie Brown's inspiration brings his friends together to decorate and make the tree work. Love is what a yellow personality uses to fix almost everything.

Other characters that will help us remember yellow personalities.

Belle, from *Beauty and the Beast*, is a yellow personality. She always sees the best in everyone, including the Beast. She wants to help and understand.

Another classic cartoon character is Cinderella. She wants to please everyone. Cinderella wants to go to the ball, but doesn't want to create a problems with her stepmother.

What words do yellow personalities use?

Yes, just listen to children talk. Each color personality has its own set of unique words that will give us hints. If children are a yellow personality, these words will naturally show up in their conversations:

- Love.
- Please.
- Nice.
- Help.
- Together.
- Caring.
- Safe.

- Encourage.
- Feelings.
- Service.
- Team.
- Together.
- Worry.
- Polite.

Some real-life examples of yellow personalities.

Sarah has a yellow personality. Every morning it takes a few hundred hugs to say goodbye to her mother when it's time for school. Her best friend is Amber. Why? Because Amber needs a friend. Sarah can't stand anyone being lonely.

John is a yellow personality. At school, he helps all his friends with their homework. He worries about their grades. Ask John, "How did your day go?" He will reply, "It was a great day. I helped two people with their math today. Now I think they understand."

Jane willingly shares her toys with friends and enjoys watching them play. She will dig around the toy bin to find the best toys to make sure everyone has something to play with. How yellow is that?

Cindy is nine years old. She has three younger brothers. Cindy is mommy's helper. She babysits, comforts, settles disputes, tidies up, and even changes the youngest's diapers. Responsibility and caring are second nature to her.

Tim worries that the new kid in his class doesn't have any friends. He wants everyone to feel happy and belong. He will always offer the chair next to him to make sure everyone finds a place to sit.

But what about the parents?

Yes, as parents, we could be a yellow personality. That would make communicating with our yellow personality child easy. We would see the world the same way.

Some examples or hints that we might be a yellow parent?

- We have a job such as a kindergarten school teacher, a social worker, a massage therapist, or a customer service representative. And, we love our work.
- We enjoy fundraising, charity projects and volunteering.
- We attend school meetings and community meetings. We enjoy meeting people and assisting in their goals.

Communicating is easy when everyone speaks the same language with the same view of the world.

"I want a cookie."

Yellow personalities want to avoid rejection and confrontation. You will notice they are usually soft-spoken. They are less direct. They will ask questions in a roundabout way instead of a very direct question.

For example, "I am feeling hungry. What do we have to eat?" Or, "I only need a little snack, do we have something like a cookie?"

Yellow personalities won't issue the command, "I want a cookie … NOW!" They are much more subtle.

Baking cookies.

The yellow personality child loves to bake cookies with Mom. It is a fun, bonding activity. This is a chance to feel great about helping and contributing. Expect a pleasant parent/child experience, rich with conversation and viewed as a combined effort. Yellow personalities love being part of a team.

The best part about making cookies?

Sharing the cookies, of course!

The biggest reward for the yellow personalities? When they see the smiles of people enjoying their homemade cookies.

Let's go to the opera!

Our yellow personality child appreciates the quality time with us. We can expect a well-behaved child, listening and behaving like an adult. Here is an opportunity for the yellow child to show maturity. Our patient yellow personality child is the perfect opera companion.

And even if they don't love the opera experience, they will still smile and be happy to just be with you.

HOW TO INTERACT WITH THE YELLOW PERSONALITY.

Remember the magic yellow word, "help." Not only will this word get their attention, it will also motivate them into action quickly.

The word "help" gets the yellow personalities' attention every time. For a moment, let's pretend we are a yellow personality. Just listen to the following phrases and see if these phrases attract our attention:

- "Can you help?"
- "I need help."
- "Will you help?"
- "Can I get some help?"
- "Please help."
- "I could use some help."
- "Do you know what would be a big help?"

Now that we have our child's attention, we add our request. For example: "Can you help me clean up these toys?"

Or, "Mommy needs help today. Could you help me clean your room?"

Being part of a team resonates with the yellow personalities.

"Help" is good, but here is an even better word.

We know the magic word "help" will get a yellow personality's attention. Now, there is another word that will make our request even more irresistible. Simply add the word "together."

Yellow personalities love doing things together. They love being part of a team. Remember, they get personal satisfaction from helping and from team activities.

Now, let's rephrase our previous request:

"Can you help me clean up these toys? We can do this together."

Here are a few more examples:

"Can you help me? I need help with this laundry. We can do this together."

"Do you know what would be a big help? If you would put away the dishes quickly, then we can make a fun dinner together."

"I could use some help. Can you clean your room? Then I can vacuum your room and we can go get ice cream together."

"If you help your teachers by getting your homework assignments done for school, we could spend time together by…"

"Do you know what would be a big help? Getting your homework done so that we can spend some quality time together."

Magic.

Discipline?

Yellow personalities normally don't need discipline. They are the best-behaved children one can imagine. Yes, they are responsible from an early age. And because they care about other people, their choices are very mature.

But when yellow personalities need discipline, what do they understand?

Yellow personalities want to please. They don't want to disappoint their parents or friends. This is a huge motivating factor in their behavior. Disappointing someone is the worst punishment possible for a yellow personality.

Going to one's room for "timeout" is easy. Even withholding privileges does not faze the yellow personality. But, disapproval from a parent or friend is excruciating punishment.

Bonding.

Yellow children value relationships. Any time spent with our yellow personality children is quality time. Here are some activities that build a better relationship with our yellow personality children.

- Shopping together.

- Preparing meals together.

- Playtime together. Any game is okay, as long as the parent participates.

- Discussing the activities of the day. Make sure to ask "how they feel" about the day's events.

- Even routine duties and everyday chores are great, when we participate with our children.

WHAT IS THE BLUE PERSONALITY?

Think action. Think excitement. Think fun. Children with blue personalities are in constant motion. Their minds are going 100 mph in several directions at the same time. And focus? No. Every new shiny object shortens their attention span.

A good way to remember the blue personality is with these words:

- Exciting.
- Dance.
- Explore.
- "Ants in the pants."
- Adventure.
- Trying everything new.
- Act first.
- Entertain.
- Fun.
- Play.
- Sing.
- New.
- Thrilling.
- Busy.
- Party.
- Try.
- Trip. ("Trip! We are going someplace new? Let's go now!")

Another way to remember the blue personality is to visualize examples in our minds. Here are some classic examples of blue personalities:

- Bugs Bunny. Always looking for a good time.

- SpongeBob SquarePants. Short attention span and focus on fun.

- Snoopy, the dog from the comic strip, Peanuts. He was always on an adventure, imagining new stories, or looking for fun. Remember Snoopy's happy dance? Or pretending to battle the "Red Baron" while sitting on his dog house?

- Pinkie Pie from My Little Pony. She's always the life of the party.

- Daffy Duck.

- Goofy. He just wandered forward through life with a perpetual smile on his face. Blue personalities are happy.

- Yogi Bear. Always testing the boundaries and having adventures.

- Ernie and the Cookie Monster from Sesame Street. Exciting people.

- The Road Runner was always active and enjoying his life. Wile E. Coyote's constant desire to catch him was just a game to the Road Runner.

- Shaggy and Scooby-Doo. Fun, adventure and laughs.

Blue personalities are full of energy. They can go full-out all day long, and they never seem to need time to recharge. Yes, this means no rest for the parents. They will go at 100% speed until the gas tank is empty. Then they collapse. We won't find a blue personality quietly lying in bed waiting to go to sleep. Unless the blue personality is exhausted, their minds will prevent them from sleeping. They want to talk. They want to do things. They just can't sleep until every ounce of energy is gone.

We see blue personalities everywhere. Why? Because they are active. Notice the toddler at the mall who stops at every store to dance to the music. We know that the parents of that blue personality are in for 15 more years of hyperactivity.

Watch for children who love to bounce on the chairs and sofa while screaming and laughing at the top of their lungs.

Our daughter, Ella, loves music. There is music in her head all the time. So from the early crawling stages, she swayed with the music. And now? She still doesn't walk. She skips, dances, and jumps all the way to her next destination.

Blue personalities are natural talkers, and they talk directly.

For example, this is a conversation with our daughter, Ella:

"Can I have a cookie?"

"No."

"How about just two cookies?"

"No. No cookies."

"Can I have three cookies if I smile?"

"Smiling is nice, but no cookies. Dinner is soon."

"If I ate just one cookie, it wouldn't spoil my dinner."

"Okay, but we are giving you just one cookie, okay?"

"Yes. Thank you. I can have the other cookies for dessert if I finish my meal."

And so the negotiations continue. Blue personalities don't seem to take rejection personally, especially about cookies. The blue personality child will just keep asking for cookies in different ways. Eventually, they grind down the resistance of their parents. We know. Verbal conflict is just a discussion for them.

At least the requests are direct. Blue personalities have no problem being direct with their questions.

Baking cookies.

Well, this is fun at first, but only briefly.

The blue personality might start off by saying, "We are going to make cookies? Yes! Hold on, I need to go put on my apron … and get my doll, oh, and she will need her apron on because she wants to make cookies too!"

The fast, ever-changing focus of the blue personality is quickly bored with the cookie-baking routine. Measuring the first few cups of flour was fun, but now we need new, more exciting stimulation. Trying to keep the blue child focused through the steps of baking cookies feels like a lost cause.

Instead of scolding and shouting, "Stay focused!" … maybe we can make the baking experience more interesting, more interactive. Or, we can accept the reality that our child will be elsewhere in five minutes. Of course our blue personality child will fly through the kitchen every few minutes to check on the progress of "our" cookies.

When baking cookies stops being fun, the blue personality child will seek other activities to fill the need for fun.

And finally, which color child will eat the most cookies? Yes! The blue personality child! Eating cookies is fun.

Let's go to the opera!

The blue personality child? Oh, where do we start?

Going to the opera? This sounds exciting. Someplace new. New experiences to enjoy. However, sitting through a boring opera is impossible for the blue personality. The child can't talk, can't dance, and has to sit quietly through the performance.

Sit quietly? No, this would never happen. The buzzing energy of the blue personality child will be a constant stress to the parent. Even the most polite blue child will be asking for different activities. "Can we go and get a drink?" Or, "When can we get up and go somewhere?" Or, "What are we going to do next?" Or, "Can I play games on your phone now?"

Now, a rock concert is the perfect outing for the blue personality. Scream, talk, sing, dance, run, cheer, refreshments, new friends, be wild, constant new inputs …

More examples of a blue personality child.

Do you remember Dory, the blue tang fish from the *Finding Nemo* movie?

Oh, she was such a blue personality. This happy-go-lucky fish wanted to make friends, and could make friends with anybody she met. She was the friendliest fish in the ocean. Happy, happy, happy.

A chance for fun? Dory would be the first to volunteer. Even when the sharks ask for volunteers, she raises her fin and shouts, "Pick me! Pick me!"

Focus? Never.

Dory's attention was constantly changing to something new. She would forget where she was going. Dory couldn't even remember that Nemo was her friend.

Her comical quote in the movie summed up her short attention span. She said, "Short-term memory loss? It runs in my family, or at least I think it does."

Blue personalities are action people. They are ready for action before they know what to do! In the movie, Dory even thinks that she knows another language. Ever seen a fish try to speak whale? Not even close, so she tries to speak louder. In her mind she thinks she can speak whale. You have to give her credit for trying.

Dory's best characteristic was that she tried to cheer people up whenever possible. She will try to cheer people up so that she will have a happy person to play with. Why not do it while singing! And celebrate? Why not? Blue personalities love a party.

The Genie from the movie, *Aladdin*.

Fast-talking and hyperactive? The Genie from Aladdin. The Genie was funny and entertaining. Always quick with jokes and songs. Plus, trapped in a lamp alone for 10,000 years was pure torture for a blue personality. Nothing to do!

The blue personalities are natural comedians, entertainers, and are very social.

Blue personalities are excited about being excited … and happy about that!

Even the simplest item or task can bring excitement and fun. Ask, "Do you want a peanut butter and jelly sandwich?"

Even that can be exciting, even though the blue personality had that very same sandwich five days in a row. Blue personalities are happy being happy. Maybe their short attention spans allow them to leave drama in the past.

Remember, add these words to our vocabulary when dealing with blue personalities. Add "fun," or "new," or "exciting," and they will respond with, "Let's do it!"

We used to tell Ella the itinerary for the day. Now we find it easier to just say, "Ready to have some fun?"

Better results. Less explanation.

Natural entertainers.

Yes, if there is an empty stage, the blue personalities want to perform. Even if no one is listening, they will take the stage. Watch the blue personalities grab their "air microphones" and start entertaining their imaginary audiences.

And don't worry about matching outfits. As long as their clothes have bright colors, they aren't too worried about the matching ensemble look. Bright, colorful, and fun.

Let's go to the game.

Blue personalities get excited about their friends having fun. Sure they can participate, but they can have fun watching and cheering too. It is not about the score of the game. It is about the cheering or the music during the timeout.

Afterwards, the blue personalities may not remember who won the game, but they can remember which songs were played on the PA system. Or, they can remember the fun dances the cheerleaders did. Maybe the most exciting part of the game was the order of chicken fingers with fries. Or maybe the giant kids' drink with the cartoon character on the souvenir cup. They had fun. They will remember the experiences that were important to them.

Don't judge a book by its cover.

This is weird. Yes, our daughter Ella is quite blue. However, take her to a museum and you would be certain she is a green personality.

She will methodically study every exhibit making sure she does not miss a single thing. For Ella, learning and reading the fascinating details is fun.

Children are not 100% of only one color personality. They may have bits of other color personalities also. We are complex human beings.

When one color is dominant, it is quite easy to understand things from our child's viewpoint. However, a child could be a blue personality, but also care a lot about other children (yellow personality). This gets even more fun as we continue our journey into the color personalities.

Are you a blue personality?

Just ask yourself, "What do I enjoy doing in my free time?"

If you enjoy activities, concerts, parties, team sports, travel, talking endlessly with friends … that is a hint. You might be a blue personality.

If you take action, even before you have directions, you might be a blue personality.

Short attention span? Get bored easily? A hundred thoughts going through your mind while you are multitasking feverously … yes, that is pretty blue.

Someone has to be the "life of the party." Why not you? Why can't you be the one to liven up the party?

If you are a blue personality, you totally understand your blue personality child. I do. As Ella's mom, I am so blue. I can't stop adding multiple projects to my day, even though my schedule is already overbooked. Hey, I have 3,261 emails in my inbox, but I am not worried. I will get to them … maybe.

Ella and I whiz through life at a breakneck speed, and we enjoy every minute of it. We let my husband, Keith, take care of the details. More about him later.

HOW TO INTERACT WITH THE BLUE PERSONALITY.

Nothing can be more unexciting than doing laundry. Boring. Blue personalities would rather have fun. Laundry is low on the fun list.

Instead of organizing clothes, hanging up clothes, or sorting laundry, what would you expect a true blue personality to do?

Yes, throw the dirty clothes in a pile in the corner. Or, have a pile of laundry around their hamper from all the missed "basket" shots. Blue personality children might even throw the clean clothes in a corner instead of carefully hanging and folding each item. Unless the parents are blue personalities, there will be conflict on how to get blue personalities to do boring chores.

So instead of stress, here is how I, Ella's father, decided to get laundry done at our house.

Asking, telling, yelling, hoping … all bad strategies for motivating the blue personality. None of those strategies sound like fun. So instead, we play a game that gets Ella's clothes put away properly and quickly.

We start by asking her, "Want to have some fun?" Of course, you know her answer. Then we do this. We are going to make putting her laundry away a fun game, one item at a time.

Step #1: We pile all of her clean laundry in the middle of the room. (If it was up to Ella, the pile would just stay there, as she would rather be having fun.)

Step #2: Get out the toy mini-hockey stick.

Step #3: With my toy hockey stick, I fling the first article of clothing at Ella. While that piece of laundry is flying through the air, I shout, "Shirt!" or "Shorts!" or whatever that flying piece of clothing is.

Step #4: Ella has to catch the flying laundry and put it away in the proper closet or drawer location as fast as she can. Speed is important to blue personalities. If Ella is too slow, more articles of clothing will come faster. This causes uncontrollable laughter, and we have to reset, and then continue the game.

Yes, this process takes longer to put the laundry away, but she loves the game.

If you want to motivate a blue personality, then find a way to make it fun.

Want to make it even more fun?

Add music! Add a reward! Add difficulty by having her sing a song, while dancing on one foot, while catching the laundry ...

Yes, this is almost too easy. Everyone wins. Ella has fun, and we get her to put away her laundry.

"Clean your room!"

To the blue personality, we could say, "Let's play a game. You and I are going to play the 'clean the room game.'" Game? That sounds like fun. The blue is already in the room ready to play.

The secret formula for blue personalities?

First, get their attention.

Second, be interesting.

Third, communicate.

Here is how this works.

Step one, get their attention. Remember that blue personality children are thinking hundreds of thoughts a minute. New thoughts and flashy objects are pulling their minds in different directions.

Step two, be interesting. Think about movie trailers or radio commercials. Use lots of blue personality words such as fun, exciting and awesome.

Step three, get to the point… quickly. Talk quickly before they get distracted. You've already captured their attention.

If we are asking the blue personality to do homework, they might have already forgotten the first half of our sentence, and are now running to play outside. They might not even hear our entire sentence. But, if we are able to get their attention, let's make it fun and get to the point. This way we will have a better success rate.

Here is an example for homework:

"Yo, Ben! I've got the coolest idea. Get your homework done now. Then you and I can play videogames together."

Discipline.

Easy. Disciplining a blue personality can be as simple as taking away the fun. The classic "if" and "then" works very well with a blue.

Here are some example,

"If you don't eat all your dinner, then you can't play with your toys."

"If you don't finish your homework, then we can't go to the mall together."

"If you can't clean up your room in time, then we can't go to the birthday party."

Remember, fun is the big motivator for a blue personality. All we need to do is to take away the fun and we will keep the blue personality on track.

Bonding.

Blue personality children don't need as much together time with their parents. They want to explore and experience new things.

Now, blue personality children are very social. They love being around others instead of being alone. So don't expect them to play quietly in their room for hours.

Since "action" is the blue personalities' middle name, our bonding activities might include:

- Going to an action movie.
- Playing video games at the local pizzeria.
- Practicing their favorite sport together.
- Just going anywhere new.
- Visiting amusement parks.
- Riding bicycles.
- Getting out of the house to any outdoor activity.
- Driving them back and forth to visit their favorite friends.
- Crazy-time, just being silly.

WHAT IS THE RED PERSONALITY?

Just think about the children who:

- Want to take charge.
- Demand to be the boss.
- Want to be #1.
- Want to be right and never wrong.
- Are self-starters.
- Desire to achieve and measure their results.
- Want to do things themselves without their parents' help or guidance.
- View every activity as a competition.
- Stand on top of the merry-go-round at recess and tell all the other children what they should be doing.

Well, maybe a bit exaggerated, but we get the point. Red personalities are driven and have strong wills. Just try to reason with a mad and upset red personality child. We all know how that score ends.

Red personality child: 1

Parents: 0

Parents lose every time. The strong-willed red personalities get their way in the end.

How to recognize a red personality.

It is easier to remember when we can associate the strong red personality traits with people. So here are a few examples:

- Lucy from the comic strip Peanuts. A natural leader, not a follower.
- G.I. Joe. Definitely a leader.
- Wile E. Coyote who chased the Road Runner in every episode. Persistent and never wanted to give up.
- Fonzie from Happy Days. The coolest, most confident person in the show.
- The Park Ranger who tried to keep Yogi Bear within the boundaries.
- Teenage Mutant Ninja Turtles. They were always fighting the villains.
- Foghorn Leghorn, the aggressive Looney Tunes rooster, who protects the chickens.
- Miss Piggy from *The Muppets*. Yes, she was always in charge and demanded results. She always had to be the center of attention.
- Mighty Mouse. Always the best.
- The Beast, from *Beauty and the Beast*. Passionately felt he was right … always.
- The Transformers. Heroes of good versus evil.

Since our red personality children have a built-in drive to be on top, these are our future athletic champions and center-stage stars. They naturally enjoy the discipline it takes to perform at their highest level.

Watch for these words from red personalities.

- In charge.
- Win.
- First place.
- The best.
- Boss.
- The leader.

- Powerful.
- Strong.
- Score.
- Number one.
- Champion.

What happens when two red personalities get together?

Just listen to the song that goes, "Anything you can do I can do better ... I can do anything better than you. No, you can't. Yes, I can. No, you can't. Yes, I can..."

Try to imagine two red personalities having a conversation. It might sound something like this:

Red #1: "I got straight A's in school this semester."

Red #2: "Oh yeah? I got all A+s and in all honor classes."

Red #1: " My mom is taking me out to eat to celebrate."

Red #2: "My mom is buying me a restaurant."

Red #1: "This summer I am going to Mexico."

Red #2: "Oh did you go parasailing? I went parasailing."

Red #1: "My parents discovered and built Mexico."

Red #1: "I'm the best player on my soccer team."

Red #2: "I'm the best player on my football team. Football is a harder sport."

Red #1: "Oh yeah? Well, I also play baseball."

Red #2: "I am pretty sure my family owns all the sports leagues."

The desire to be #1 and the desire to compete will dominate the discussion when two red personalities talk.

But this interaction is different when a red, competitive personality talks with a blue, "have fun" personality.

Ella is a blue personality. She just wants to have fun. Here is Ella having a conversation with her red personality classmate, Sharon.

Sharon: "I got 17 pieces of work done today, Ella. How many have you finished?"

Ella: "Good for you. What is the teacher doing over there? What is that big styrofoam ball doing with a stick in it?"

Sharon: "Ella, you are not paying attention!"

Too late. Ella is already outside playing.

How do red personality children see the world?

Red personalities love to achieve. Personal achievement is everything. Measuring results and comparing the results with others ... that is the red personality way of life. A typical red conversation?

"Yesterday I did three more push-ups than everyone in my class. And Johnny's push-ups weren't right. He didn't go all the way down like he should."

Reds are constantly motivated to achieve. If they like their studies, they will push themselves to be the best. If they like their sport, they will practice every day to improve.

Let's talk cookies.

Red personalities are definitely direct in their communication. For example:

"Can I have a cookie now?"

"I want a cookie now."

"I am hungry. I need a cookie now."

They don't have time to be indirect or give hints. They will tell you what they want and when they want it.

Red personalities will make direct requests. We won't have to guess what they are feeling. They are not being rude. They are simply communicating in their own style.

And conflict? Red personalities don't mind conflict. They focus on getting what they want. Conflict is negotiation, not rejection to them.

Red personality: "Can I have a cookie now?"

Dad: "No."

Red personality: "But I need a cookie now."

Dad: "No."

Red personality: "I didn't have a cookie yesterday, so I should get a cookie now."

Dad: "No. A cookie will spoil your meal."

Red personality: "I am very hungry now. I need a cookie. I am so hungry that I will still have plenty of room to eat dinner."

Dad: "No."

Red personality: "I deserve a cookie. I have been good all day."

Dad: "No. No cookies before dinner."

Red personality: "I promise to eat dinner. Can I have my cookie now?"

Dad: "Okay, but don't tell your mother
I gave you a cookie."

Baking cookies.

The red personality? Oh my. Stay out of the way.

The red personality child wants to control and perform the entire baking sequence herself. Don't help. Don't assist. Don't give instructions or directions. Suggestions aren't welcomed. Just watch the independent child do things her way. This is her show, and you can only watch.

Plus, guess who gets to pick the flavor of the cookies?

Let's go to the opera.

The red child is bored. No competition. No score.

Our red personality child throws a tantrum and demands a different activity. There will be a war of wills in the theater. This conflict will continue until the red personality child gets his or her way.

Are you a red personality?

Are you driven by results? Are you a bottom-line person? Then you might be a red personality.

Red personalities thrive in jobs where they are the manager, the boss, the person in charge of making everything right. If something needs to be completed, let the red personality be responsible.

Do you have a competitive nature? Do you thrive on recognition and accomplishment?

Well, if some of these attributes feel comfortable to you, you might be a red personality. That means communicating with our red personality child will be easy. You both speak the same language.

HOW TO INTERACT WITH THE RED PERSONALITY.

Want to motivate a red personality? Try these:

- Ribbons.
- Awards.
- Competitions.
- Recognition.
- Money.
- Challenges.

**Motivating a red personality
is almost too easy.**

Want some examples?

- Set a timer to clean the room. See if they can beat their best time.
- Remind them that their brother cleaned his room faster yesterday.

- Say, "You are pretty good at cleaning your room, but this is a big job today. I don't think you could finish cleaning your room before dinner." And the race is on! Here is the chance for the red personality to prove the parents wrong.

Bonding.

Red personalities don't need companionship as much as the yellow personalities. They focus on their personal accomplishments and goals. When we assist in their improvement and development, this counts as quality time with our red personality children.

Here are just a few examples of bonding activities with red personality children:

- Building a Lego™ fortress.
- Going to a car show to dream about new cars.
- If they play the violin, taking them to a violin concert to see a professional perform.
- If they want to grow up and become an actor, taking them to a play or musical.
- Helping them practice their favorite passion.
- Helping them make their school project not only excellent, but perfect!

Discipline.

Because of their competitive nature, red personalities value the chance to compete in events. They love to be the star. Having a chance to perform in even more events is a huge motivation to red personalities.

Red personalities have natural discipline. They can control their behavior, especially for future incentives.

Good behavior means more and better opportunities. Red personalities understand this quickly.

WHAT IS THE GREEN PERSONALITY?

Think … thinkers. Green personalities, like the yellow personalities, are quieter than other children. Green personalities are busy observing their surroundings and learning. Naturally inquisitive, they will frustrate busy parents with endless questions of why things are the way they are.

Their favorite words are:

"Why? Why? Why? Why? But why?"

This can drive parents crazy. Green personalities want to know why things are the way they are. They are logical.

Have we ever found ourselves in this one-sided conversation? The only word our child says is "why" … even after we give all the possible answers. As parents, we eventually get frustrated and end the conversation by saying, "Because I said so, that's why!"

"Why" is the most important word for the curious green personality child.

Green personalities are not very outgoing. They need time to recharge. They can take in lots of data and experiences. However, they then want quiet time to process it and make sense of it all. They want to understand what they've learned before moving on.

Do you have a well-behaved child that can entertain himself? Well, that is the green personality.

With all their quiet thinking time, green personalities can daydream a lot. They can spend hours reading or constructing Lego™ buildings and airplanes. They also might deconstruct toys to see their inner workings, how the toy is put together and why it works. Because they can be caught up in their own thoughts, interaction with other children isn't a requirement.

Green personalities carefully plan all their activities. And the words "learning something new" mean excitement for them.

Because green personalities are more logical, science and mathematics seem natural to them.

What words are commonly used by green personalities?

- Why.
- Find out why.
- Study.
- Information.
- Think.

- Directions.
- Safe.
- Proof.
- Experiment.
- How?

Here are some famous characters that are green personalities.

- Velma from *Scooby-Doo*. She could solve any mystery with her intelligence.
- Count von Count, the counting Dracula character from *Sesame Street*. Counting and having things in order made him happy.
- Mr. Spock from *Star Trek*. Logical, fewer emotions, and careful in his decisions.
- Chandler from *Friends*. His sarcastic sense of humor showed his deep thinking. And of course, Ross, with his know-it-all rationality.

"I want a cookie."

Green personalities are quieter and indirect. They won't be confrontational to get their cookie. Instead, they will use logic to get their way. The conversation might go something like this:

Green personality: "I am starting to feel hungry, but I don't want to spoil my dinner."

Mother: "Oh? What would you like to do?"

Green personality: "I probably should eat just a tiny snack. I don't want to spoil my dinner."

Mother: "Okay, what kind of snack should we get?"

Green personality: "Something small. I do want to eat my whole dinner."

Mother: "I don't know what we have that is small. Any suggestions?"

Green personality: "Maybe I should just get a cookie. Cookies are small, and won't ruin my appetite."

Mother: "Of course. Good idea. Let me get you a cookie now."

Baking cookies. The patience test.

Bake cookies with the green personality child. Everything must be measured and checked. No cookie batter can splash anywhere without stopping the process to arrange clean-up procedures. Read the directions slowly and entirely. Recheck. And if we, the parent, have a blue personality, we will want to pull out our hair in frustration and impatience.

Time to bite our tongue and go along with the slow-paced approach to baking cookies.

And forget about using words like "pinch," "dash" or "handful." The green will not understand this concept of measuring. They want exact measurements to make sure the cookies turn out right.

Learning and mastering the cookie-baking process is enjoyable for the green personalities.

Do green personalities have a natural sense of fashion?

Usually not. Of course, we are exaggerating again. Not all green personalities will fit this description. We are just trying to set up some guidelines to help us remember the different personalities.

So, for green personalities, fashion might not be the top priority in their lives. They are easy to spot. Functional clothing just makes sense to them. Chances are if they dress themselves, the clothes would not match. If was up to them, their clothing would last forever. No need to waste time on useless excursions like shopping. They would prefer for their parents to buy them the clothes, and let them know exactly what to wear.

Let's go to the opera.

Our green personality child might be bored. But, cautious and well-behaved, our green personality child will suffer through the ordeal. Good thing we brought a book or alternate activity along with us to the opera.

It would be a good idea to find a seat with a good view of the action which takes place behind the stage. The green personality will be fascinated by the workings of the stage curtain. They will observe the sides of the stage to see what the ropes control, or peek at what the backstage people are doing. They will look around to see which lights shine on the stage and make the different color combinations.

Another example of the green personality from Ella.

My friend Vicki is green. Every day she reviews and checks her papers to make sure there are no mistakes. Her goal? 100% perfection. When she writes, she uses cursive because it is faster and more efficient. Her papers and work are always organized. Before recess, she puts everything away slowly and carefully, and makes me wait, and wait, and wait. I just want to hurry up and play.

Are you a green personality?

Do you pay attention to details? Do you carefully plan and think through your decisions? Do books and computers seem more rational than erratic human behavior?

These are good signs that you might be a green personality.

What are some of the occupations where we will find an abundance of green personalities? Accountants, engineers, data processors and highly-competent videogame players.

Green personality parents relate and communicate with green personality children. Logic, detail, and future-planning scenarios make conversations easy. It might sound something like this:

"Time to go to bed. You have to get up early to go to school tomorrow."

"I have already brushed my teeth and folded my clothes. Let me play with this puzzle for ten more minutes before I go to bed."

"You don't want to feel tired when you wake up tomorrow though. Don't you think you should go to bed now?"

"I will stay awake if I go now. I would worry about finishing the puzzle. I should finish the puzzle now so that I can go to sleep without thinking about the next moves."

"Okay. Makes sense. Good luck on finishing the puzzle quickly."

"No luck needed. I researched the possible solutions already on the Internet."

Okay, maybe a bit exaggerated. But expect a steady, even conversation among green personalities. No stress.

HOW TO INTERACT WITH THE GREEN PERSONALITY.

This is the hardest color to motivate. Why? Because they won't do anything unless it makes sense.

That means everything should be thought-out and considered. Sometimes it will take forever for green personalities to make a decision. But once they make that decision, they will know it is the correct decision.

First, we must get their attention.

Here are some good attention-getting questions for green personalities:

- "Does this make sense?"
- "I wonder if you can figure this out?"
- "Is this an interesting problem to solve?"
- "Does this look perfect or does it need to be improved?"

Now we have their attention. If we are not a green personality, this seems boring. But for the green personalities, these questions are engaging. This is now a challenge. Can they figure it out?

Do you want them to put away the laundry? Ask them, "What do you think is the best way to organize these clean clothes?"

Do you want them to do their homework? Ask them, "Would you let me know when you finish your homework? Then we can plan our day for tomorrow."

Do you want them to clean their room? Ask them, "Do you think with my help, we could organize and clean this room in 15 minutes?"

Or you could just say, "Let's get your room organized." Well, maybe that won't motivate the green personalities, but at least they will understand.

Discipline a green personality.

Removing Internet access would be the ultimate punishment. Even child services might consider this "cruel and unusual punishment" for a green personality child.

Inviting a bunch of screaming, laughing, undisciplined blue personalities to play with the green personality's Lego™ collection would be torture. Not recommended.

Since green personalities are more likely to consider their actions, they take fewer chances and risks. They seldom go too far outside the boundaries. This makes discipline less of a problem with green personality children. They are more predictable.

Learning experiences are high on their list of interesting and fun things to do. Discipline is easy if it is tied to a future learning experience trip. Planning for the future is easy for them.

Bonding.

Green personalities enjoy quiet time with ... themselves. They don't require constant outside input to be happy. This quiet time with their thoughts is necessary for them to sort all of the day's input. So bringing extra stimulation into their lives by inviting more children to come and play isn't necessary.

So what do green personality children want to do? Here are some activities we can do with our green personality children:

- Helping them study. Asking test questions, explaining new concepts or helping with flash cards.

- Going to shows or museums where they can learn more about their favorite passions.

- Playing a board game.

- Assembling Lego™ sets using the instruction sheets.

- Creating a school project.

- Enjoying their hobby with you.

SO WHAT COLOR PERSONALITY IS OUR CHILD?

After reading about these four color personalities, we might be wondering, "So what color is my child?"

Our children are not 100% of one of these personalities. They won't be totally green or totally blue. But usually one of these color personalities are dominant for them.

In our case, our daughter Ella is predominantly a blue personality. However, if she is studying or doing a project she loves, you would swear she was a green personality. She gets so focused on things she likes, things that she finds to be fun.

Are you starting to see a pattern? Can you see how our children see their world in entirely different perspectives?

These four different color personalities give us a peek into how we can communicate differently and more effectively. This helps us to relate with how our children see and understand the world.

Want some help or a quick review?

Here are some broad examples of what we might notice when observing the four different color personalities. These should look pretty familiar by now.

Going on vacation.

Yellow personality: Gets excited to spend quality time with the family.

Blue personality: Gets excited. No details needed.

Red personality: Wants to brag to her friends about where they are going.

Green personality: Asks for exact details and schedule.

If you could bottle it up and sell their best qualities, it would be their:

Yellow personality: Thoughtfulness.

Blue personality: Enthusiasm.

Red personality: Leadership.

Green personality: Exactness.

Stays up late on a school night because:

Yellow personality: Worried they forgot to say goodnight to someone.

Blue personality: Thinking about everything else but school.

Red personality: Concerned about not acing a test the next day.

Green personality: Making sure everything is ready and prepared.

When receiving a compliment:

Yellow personality: Is overwhelmed with a genuine smile.

Blue personality: Does a victory touchdown dance.

Red personality: Says "I knew I would!"

Green personality: Nods his head and says a quick and quiet, "Thank you."

When playing with others:

Yellow personality: Cares about everyone getting along.

Blue personality: The more people, the merrier!

Red personality: "I will be the leader!"

Green personality: Has outlined the day with planned activities in 15-minute increments.

The Ready, Set, Go! Theory

Yellow personality: Before anything can happen, the yellow will make sure everyone is ready. They might even check to see if anyone else wants to join or if they need help. Then finally they will be ready to go together, but only when the whole group is ready.

Blue personality: "Go!" is first. Then later comes the afterthought of "Ready" and "Set," but only after the action has already taken place.

Red personality: Go! Just go! Who has time for "ready" and "set?" They are always ready and set, let's just go.

Green personality: "Ready," "set," double-check "set," check again, check to make sure I'm really "ready," check "set" again and now … start planning to "go."

When playing sports:

Yellow personality: Teamwork is fun. Enjoys the opportunity to participate as part of the team.

Blue personality: Wants the team with exciting colors and the best cheers.

Red personality: Wants to achieve and perform at the highest level. Wants to win.

Green personality: Wants to learn how to play the sport more competently.

In school:

Yellow personality: The hippie.

Blue personality: The class clown.

Red personality: The leader.

Green personality: The intellectual.

Emotions:

Yellow personality: Hugging.

Blue personality: Cheering.

Red personality: Winning.

Green personality: Still analyzing.

Toys:

Yellow personality: You can expect them to take care of and love their toys. Each toy will have a unique, lovable name.

Blue personality: With a shorter attention span and a need for constant input, they will leave an organized room of toys looking like a tornado/tsunami/ earthquake just struck.

Red personality: They claim the best toys. They might take the toys to their physical limits and occasionally break a toy.

Green personality: They can organize their toys. They will study the limits of their toys and research the accessories and alternatives to their favorite toys. Green personalities might take apart their toys just to see what's inside and figure out how they work.

Now, this is becoming more obvious.

When we figure out our child's dominant color personality, we can adjust to how they see the world. Now our communication is stronger.

Let's use motivation and discipline, for example. Of course this is an over-simplification, but it will help us focus on looking at the world from our child's viewpoint.

Yellow personality

Motivation: To help someone and feel good
about it. They are easy to motivate.

Discipline: They are crushed when we
feel disappointed.

Blue personality

Motivation: Playtime, fun, candy.

Discipline: No fun stuff. Go to your room
and be alone.

Red personality

Motivation: Put them in charge. Let them
be the leader.

Discipline: Take away things and make
them earn it back.

Green personality

Motivation: Explain the reasons why.
A chance to learn.

Discipline: A timeout in their room with
no stimulation.

One type of motivation or discipline doesn't work for every child. It is up to us as parents to be more flexible in our approach.

Our language barrier functions.
Am I speaking English?

Here is the perfect example of not speaking in our children's color personality language.

As a family, we love to travel together. Fortunately, we get the opportunity to travel to many other countries.

Often on our travels we will see an American tourist trying to communicate with a local who doesn't speak English. Usually the American tourist will start by asking a question. When the local appears not to understand, what does the American tourist do?

Speak slower. And when that doesn't work?

Speak louder. Of course being louder doesn't fix the communication problem. So what next?

Hand gestures. And when that doesn't work?

Frustration!!!

The one-sided conversation ends with confusion for both people involved. No communication occurs. Period.

Sound familiar?

When we speak in our own personality color, but not in our child's personality color, it is like trying to speak to someone who doesn't speak the same language. It simply doesn't work.

As parents we end up saying:

- "I just don't get him. Why won't he listen to me?"
- "I don't know why she won't just apply herself. I was never like that."
- "Why won't he pay attention?"
- "What was our child thinking?"
- "Why is she crying when I just told her I was disappointed?"

No matter how much we push, beg, or plead with our child, sometimes we can't communicate. Why? Because we are using techniques and words that work for our personality color, but don't work for their personality color.

Ultimately, it's not about what works for us, but rather what will work for our children that counts. We need to learn to speak their language and not just ours.

Yes, we are the ones who have to adjust our language. We are the adults. They are just children. It's a big world and they have so much to learn. We can't expect them to rigidly adjust to us.

WHAT HAPPENS IN ELLA'S LIFE.

Ella here.

Let me share with you what my life is like with the different color personalities.

As you already know, my mother is a blue personality, and my father is a green personality. I get to watch their differences every day of my life. More about them later.

Here are some of my experiences with my friends and teachers.

My class recital.

My green personality friends are the ones in the back row. They don't like to have everyone staring at them. They think, "Everyone is looking at me. Is there something wrong?" So of course, they always want to be in the background behind the others.

My red personality friends? They love to be at the front of the stage. They like to be the stars of the show. They want to be the actor with the most lines, or they want to be the first to sing or play their instrument.

Thankfully, I have yellow personality friends that help the teacher. They make the green personalities feel comfortable and help get everyone on stage in time.

But I have blue personality friends just like me. We love to perform. Even when the stage is empty we love to get up and pretend we have an audience. We just love to have fun. You can always spot the blues in the group because we are the ones who wave from the stage and say, "Hi Mom!" in the middle of the performance.

Unfortunately, we talk a lot. Our teacher always has to tell us to be quiet and be still while others are performing.

My first day of school.

Kids everywhere. Some were happy and smiling. A few were crying. The rest were running around and just being crazy.

Jeff (green personality) had a death grip on his mother's leg. He didn't want to be here with the rest of us kids.

One of the kids, Mark (blue personality), was swinging his backpack in one hand, his lunch in the other, pretending to be a merry-go-round. The other children were ducking and laughing.

Jerry (red personality) was looking through the pencils and other supplies to find the best ones and put them all in his desk.

But Diana (yellow personality) found a pack of pens that Jerry missed. She brought Jerry one of the pens and smiled.

This made Jerry happy. Then Jerry started shouting, "This is my desk, this is my chair, these are my books …"

We had fun the first day of school. And we were loud. I am not sure the teacher had a good time. Not many children were listening. I couldn't wait for day two of school. I would meet more new friends to play with.

Easter egg hunt.

Molly came to visit me. She is a yellow personality. My parents were taking us to the park for an Easter egg hunt.

On the way to the park we talked about how much fun we were going to have. Since Molly is a yellow personality, and I am a blue personality, neither of us worried about the contests or winning. No talk of how many Easter eggs we were going to collect. We just wanted to have a good time.

When the hunt started, Molly spent a lot energy cheering me as I ran. She didn't spend much time looking for Easter eggs for herself.

When we found all the eggs, it was Molly's idea to trade eggs with other children. She thought this would help everyone be happier. They could trade for the colored eggs and the miniature toys they wanted. One girl found something that she liked out of Molly's bag. Of course she checked with me to see if I wanted it first.

At the end of the Easter egg hunt, they announced, "Check your eggs. Some of the eggs have golden tokens that you can use to get an extra toy."

Molly had an egg with a token. She made sure that she picked a toy that wasn't just for her, but something that we could both play with.

I like having fun with yellow personalities.

All the colors at once.

One day at school my friend, Michelle, was working on her science assignment.

Michelle is a green personality. She had a piece of paper taped high on the wall and a pad of ink. Her assignment was to measure and graph how high she could jump.

She placed her fingertips on the ink pad, then she would jump and touch the paper to leave her fingerprints. Michelle continued to do this over and over. Why? Because after each jump, she noticed her results were a little different. This took a long time as she would measure and record her results after every jump.

She continued jumping because she wanted to get a consistent result with each jump. Green personalities are like that.

Soon Ryan (red personality) came up to see what Michelle was doing. He wanted to try. Even though he is much shorter than Michelle, he kept trying to jump higher. He wanted to leave his fingerprints higher on her paper. He always wants to win.

And finally, when Michelle finished collecting her data, she struggled to reach her paper taped high on the wall. But no worries. Sarah (yellow personality) came with a chair for her to stand on. Sarah is always helping everyone at school.

After a while I decided to start making fingerprint art on the extra paper (of course I asked my teacher first). I was having fun making cool designs with my fingerprints. But when Michelle saw what I was doing she said, "Ella, you can't do art today! It isn't Wednesday and we do art on Wednesday!" I guess she just didn't like changing the rules.

I love our field trips.

My school takes a lot of field trips.

You can always tell which students are the yellow personalities. They make sure no one is left behind, and that everyone holds hands with their partner. They will tell the teacher that Eddie forgot his lunch, or spilled his drink and needs another one.

For us blue personalities, field trips are fun. They are much better than staying inside our classroom all day. That can be boring. For us, field trips are fun and exciting. They are better than recess!

Maybe we run around too much, cause problems, or talk too much. But we love the new experiences. We love seeing something new.

The red personalities want to be the boss. They are always first in line. They like telling everyone what they should do or where they should be standing. They tell us everything they know about what we are doing. It is probably good they are first in line.

The green personalities? They love field trips too. They pay attention. They take notes. And on the way back from the field trip they explain to the rest of us all the stuff we missed and didn't pay attention to.

Our field trip to the Children's Museum.

At the Houston Children's Museum, there is a section that is a make-believe town. When you enter the town you receive a debit card to earn money and spend money. In this town you have to work at a business to earn money and there is a store to buy groceries. It's just like a real town, except kid-sized.

On our school field trip this town didn't exactly work like it should. A group of kids started pretending to be bank robbers. They pretended to steal money and food from the store. Then they pretended to drive away in a fake car to escape. Soon other kids started pretending to be the police chasing the robbers. It was funny to see that most of the robbers who were breaking the rules were blue personalities. And the police? They were the red and green personalities.

That was a really fun trip!

The Health Museum field trip.

The Children's Health Museum was also a great field trip. We learned lots of great things on this trip. The best exhibit? The "learning about hearing" section.

There was a decibel-measuring booth. The goal of the booth was to go inside and scream. On the outside was a meter to show how loud you could scream. The red personalities enjoyed going into the booth to scream and see who could scream the loudest. They kept taking turns going in to try and scream louder then the person before them.

The green personalities were outside watching the meter and measuring the differences. The blue personalities were laughing and some even screamed too, even though we were on the outside of the booth. Some of the yellow personalities offered to go in the booth to help make it louder. Other yellow personalities were saying, "Don't go in there. You will hurt your ears."

Working on school group projects.

When I work on projects at school, I am careful to remember the color personality of my partner.

If my partner is a yellow personality, it will be easy and fun doing the project. We will work together. We will help each other on the hard parts. We usually take turns writing the project. Nobody will be the boss, but my yellow personality partner will make sure that we finish the project on time.

Once the teacher assigned a red personality partner for our project. That was a completely different experience. I knew right away that she wanted to be the leader and the one in charge. But I had ideas about what we should do for the project as well. The only way I could make this work was to begin by listening and agreeing. I let her know that she had good ideas. If I tried to change things or didn't agree, it would cause a big explosion.

So I listened. And listened. And listened. When she finally finished, this was my chance to get my ideas into the project.

Since red personalities feel best when they are in charge, I just asked questions and let her answer.

For example, when working on a dolphin research project, my red personality partner said, "We should write about where they live and what they eat." I said, "That's great. You are good at researching those. Do you think I should research dolphin behavior?" Of course she felt like she was still in charge and agreed to the idea right away.

Now, when I work with another blue personality on a project … oh my! It can sometimes be a disaster.

One time my blue personality partner and I were writing a book about monkeys. We made a huge popup, unfortunately the popup ripped because we didn't know how to make it properly. We didn't get upset. Instead, we started writing jokes about the animals in our paper. We had so much fun that we completely forgot to write about our research. I know working with another blue personality means that I will need to stay on task and get our work done. Getting distracted is too easy.

When I work with a green personality, everything has to be perfect. I know they will need everything to be exact, correct and neat. The green personality will want me to write in cursive and to be neat with no mistakes.

Once I was working with a green personality and I made a small mistake. My partner did not like this at all. She lost her mind actually. Gee, it was only one little mistake. She wanted to start writing everything over because you could see the eraser marks. Write everything over? That's not fun. That's boring.

Teachers have personality colors too... and I use this to my advantage.

My piano teacher is a blue personality. I look forward to my lessons because I know we are going to have fun. This makes it so easy to learn. Maybe that is why I love playing the piano. It is always fun.

One of my classroom teachers is a green personality. I know when I turn in work it has to not only be correct but also neat with good handwriting. She will not accept work if it is only half-done. She won't even look at the work if you forget to put your name at the top. One of my classmates tried to turn in work with drawing on it. She was not happy about this. Even though he had the correct answers and everything was complete, she was not happy with the doodling.

I learned not to doodle on work I give to this green personality teacher.

Our school "fun run" experience.

Our school's "fun run" raises money for our school. Of course all the yellow personalities get involved. This is good. We get more money for the school.

The yellow personalities are holding hands and singing, or they are busy cheering for the kids who are still running. The blue personalities? We seem to get distracted off to the side dancing to the music and talking to the other kids by the water. We forget other people are running.

The red personalities were running to seeing who could do more laps. And the green personalities were counting the laps, making sure our school got credit for every lap.

But what about my parents?

My mom is blue, just like me! This is so much fun. We get to start things, and then start more things, and try even more different things. Having a blue personality mom is fun!

How do I know my mom is a blue personality? Well, she told me this conversation she had with her mom.

* * *

My parents were not blue. They didn't understand my perspective. Growing up I can remember my mom always saying, "Where is that girl? Oh look. There she is over there dancing. Ugh!"

Conversations with my red personality mom went something like this:

Mom: "Get over here and clean your room."

Me: Not paying attention.

Mom: "I bet you can't get this room clean faster than I can clean my kitchen."

Me: "You are right mom. I am going to go ride my bike now."

Mom: "Arrrggghhh!"

These conversations left my mom frustrated and irritated. She rarely could motivate me to clean my room.

What was the problem? Competition to see who can clean a room faster works for red personality mothers, but doesn't work for blue personality daughters. What motivated her did nothing for me.

* * *

But what about my dad? Well, he is such a green personality. He plans and plans. Then, my mom and I ruin the plans with new, fun ideas. I know he gets a bit frustrated when he calmly explains things to me. Why? Because I run off to do something new while he is still talking. Or sometimes I interrupt him because I can't wait to hear everything, I'm ready to go.

I am so glad my parents taught me about the color personalities. It helps me to understand my friends and teachers. I use the color personalities to make my life easier. It even helps me with my parents. I just talk with them and usually get my way. Sometimes I am surprised when they don't realize what I am doing. I hope they don't catch on soon.

WHAT HAPPENS WHEN THE COLOR WORLDS OF CHILDREN COLLIDE??

Let's watch different color personality children as they react to each other's view of the world. This should be fun.

The red personality and the blue personality.

Sharon is a red personality. She needs somebody to play with. So she calls Ella, our blue daughter. The conversation goes something like this:

Sharon: "Want to come over to my house?"

Ella: "What are we going to do?"

Sharon: "I will let you know when you get here."

Ella: "Will we have fun?"

Sharon: "I will be in charge. Just come over."

Ella: "Okay, sounds like fun."

Sharon likes the conversation. It was quick and to the point. Ella on the other hand, wants to keep talking, even though they will see each other shortly.

Once they are together...

> **Ella:** "What have you been doing today? Did you have fun?"
>
> **Sharon:** "I read two books, swam 45 minutes straight, and I'm the fastest freestyle swimmer on my swim team."
>
> **Ella:** "Was it fun?"
>
> **Sharon:** "Yes, of course. I bet I can run to that tree and back faster then you can."
>
> **Ella:** "I bet you could. Go ahead, I'll cheer for you."
>
> **Sharon:** "Ugh!"

Competition is not a high priority for Ella, but Sharon loves to win at everything. She often gets frustrated with Ella for not wanting to join in on the competition. But, they always have fun together because Sharon gets to be the boss in charge of the play date.

If Sharon wants to change activities, all she has to do is use the magic phrase, "Want to have some fun?" Chances are Ella will go along with it.

A red personality with a yellow personality.

Nothing can be more opposite than the red and yellow personalities. The red personality wants to be in charge, and the yellow personality doesn't want to make decisions. They certainly complement each other. There is barely a conflict.

The yellow personalities enjoy making the other person happy. No decisions have to be made, so they happily go along with the flow.

The red personality will decide what to eat and what to do. Yellow personalities seem to adjust to their wishes. Even if they don't like the recommended food, they will eat the food and smile. Why voice a different opinion when you can make people happy by going along with everything?

These two almost always get along. Some say that the yellow personality is the only personality that can put up with the red personality. Fast-forward years from now, and these two will probably get married.

The green personality with a yellow personality.

This is easy. Both personalities are indirect and don't like conflict. The conversation might go something like this:

Green personality: "What would you like to?"

Yellow personality: "Whatever you want to do."

Green personality: "Okay, let's learn about reptiles."

Yellow personality:	"Sounds great. Do you enjoy learning about reptiles?"
Green personality:	"Of course. They are very interesting. Many different types." (This is massive excitement for the green personality.)
Yellow personality:	"Okay, let's learn about reptiles."
Green personality:	"Let's start with these books here."

The rest of the day the yellow personality listens and watches the green personality study reptiles. If the green personality ever cracks a smile, the yellow personality feels great. This is an easy pairing.

The green personality with the blue personality.

These personalities are opposite. Listening to them communicate is too funny. You have to smile as it sounds like two totally different conversations happening at the same time.

Blue personality:	"Ready to have some fun?"
Green personality:	"It depends. What exactly are we going to do?"
Blue personality:	"We could jump, spin around in circles, go to a movie, play a board game, kick a ball, ride bikes …"
Green personality:	"Wait, so what exactly are we going to do first?"

Blue personality: "I am not sure. I think we should… oh, did you know that I can go one minute without blinking?"

Green personality: "Ummmm, so are we going to not blink? I am so confused, what are we going to do now?"

Blue personality: "One time I tried not blinking but then I had to sneeze. It was so funny. I thought my eyeballs would pop out."

Green personality: "Okay, so we are going to try not to blink. I don't understand why we are doing this."

This can go on and on until the green suggests something interesting that will get the blue personality to focus. When that happens? Magic. They have fun and are organized at the same time. We call it "calculated fun."

The green personality with the red personality.

These two personalities always think they are correct. So, they will get along if they both believe it is the right decision.

If they are working together on a class project, look out! This will be the most over-the-top, intricately-displayed, super project of all times.

The green personality will overwhelm us with information, facts, and statistics. For example, if the project is about a country, we will know everything about the currency, the food, the economy, the government, the types of soil found, its ancient history, and a whole lot more.

The red personality will make sure it is the best presentation ever. We will know why this is the number one country of all time. Everything will be the best. And, the red personality will insist that their pictures (as the creators of this wonderful project) be the center of the project.

Maybe the green personality did most of the work. However, the red personality will take full credit for it. Red personalities know they are the smartest people in the class, even though their grades may not show it. The school's grading system is all wrong.

MOOD CHANGES AND CHAMELEONS.

Do children have moods? Of course. And they can change almost instantly.

One moment they are singing and dancing and having a great time. The next moment they are throwing a tantrum because they are right and we, as parents, are wrong.

What do we have to do as parents? We need to adjust. We need to be a chameleon so that we can communicate with our children with the appropriate moods. This can give us the unfair advantage that we need.

For example, our blue child is skipping and singing around the playground, going from one shiny object to the next. Something catches his eyes. A ladybug. But wait, it is time to leave to go to the library. But our child is having fun!

Now, we could try communicating in the blue personality language. We could say, "Let's go to the library. That will be fun." But, our blue child is having a "green moment." He has found something fun that has captured his attention. So a better and more effective way to communicate with our child is by using the green personality language.

Maybe we can say something like, "Wow, I see you found a little ladybug. Did you know the library has lots of books about ladybugs? If we leave right now, we can find those books and you can look at all their fun pictures."

Now we have his interest. More pictures and books to look at sounds tempting. He is now running to the car, ready to go and help find books at the library. Now that was easy.

When our red personality child has a bad day.

Our red personality pre-teen comes home from a bad day at school feeling a little down. She didn't win the spelling competition. Ouch! (Remember, red personalities want to win.) Plus, she had a difficult math test and her friends ignored her today. She comes to us for a hug.

This is not the right time to use a red personality technique to get her to clean her room. Instead, we switch to a yellow personality technique. We give her a big hug and let her know we will help her clean her room … together.

MORE REAL LIFE EXAMPLES.

This is fun. The more we observe, the easier it gets. Let's look at some more experiences and see the different color personalities.

The birthday party.

Attend a six-year-old's birthday party. We will see different personalities at all their activities.

If the children are eating pizza ...

The yellow personalities:

- Make sure everyone gets the right amount and the correct pizza they wanted.
- Wait until the end to get their pizza and eat.
- Make sure everyone has a drink.
- Are happy and composed, even in the chaos of a children's birthday party.
- Are happy to help with the clean-up.

The blue personalities:

- Are excited about having pizza. Eating pizza is fun!
- Finish last because they are too busy talking and playing.
- Play with their food. Make a pizza tower/pyramid/ fort.
- Ask, "I wonder how much pizza I can put in my mouth to look like a chipmunk?"
- Entertain everyone with their off-the-wall ideas.

The red personalities:

- Have to have the perfect slice with the exact toppings.
- Talk about how much pizza they can eat in a single sitting.
- Make sure to sit in a place where they can be the center of attention.
- Tell everyone, "Make sure and come to my party on my birthday. It will be amazing."

The green personalities:

- Take forever to make a simple choice - cheese or pepperoni.
- Get frustrated when other kids get seconds without eating the crust.

- Are confused about why the blue personality kids are talking so much instead of concentrating on eating.

- Will say, "I am finished, where is the proper place to put my plate away?"

What if the birthday party was at a jumping location?

Children love trampolines. Jumping is a great way to release energy and, well … it is just fun.

But how would the different color personalities react to a trampoline birthday party?

- The yellow personalities would hold hands and jump in a group.

- The blue personalities would uncontrollably jump and scream. How close can we get to the edge? What if we jumped off the trampoline to the sandbox? Let's try bouncing on our heads!

- The red personalities would have a competition to see who could jump the highest. Please, no weaker color personalities on the trampoline during our competition.

- The green personalities would carefully pick an area to avoid bumping into the other children while calculating their jumps.

What are the natural reactions of the different color personalities to sports?

Yellow personalities? The ultimate team players. Sport is not about individual achievement. It is all about the team. The yellow personalities don't stress about the score. Any position is okay if it will help the team.

Who are the best cheerleaders? Obviously, the yellow personalities. They cheer for everyone, win or lose.

The blue personalities? Sports are a great way to focus their energy and to express themselves. Just think "fun" and watch the blue personalities enjoy the experience. Plus, sports mean more people to talk and interact with. Blues love interaction with others.

Sitting on the bench isn't fun. Extreme discipline isn't fun. Participating? Now, that's fun. Let's take the rules to the limits and try playing the sport in different ways.

Blues are the first to volunteer for activities.

What about the red personalities? No surprise here. They want to compete. They want to win. They want to set new records. Of course they want to be the captain of the team and have the most important position while playing. In baseball, they will insist on being the pitcher or the clean-up hitter. In soccer, they want to be the high-scoring forward.

We can expect the red personalities to be the highest scorers, the best tacklers, and focused on being the best. They are self-motivated and will practice daily to excel.

Red personalities are natural leaders. Expect them to boss around the rest of the team to get the best team performance possible. No problem spotting the red personalities when playing sports.

The green personalities will study all the rules before even considering playing the game. Expect them to study the sport in books, watch videos, and want to read everything before getting started. Of course they can point out everyone who breaks a rule or doesn't play fair.

Who wants to play a board game?

Yellow personalities will let everyone else have the first move on the board game. What game? It doesn't matter. Yellow personalities enjoy the time with others and make sure everyone gets their turn.

Blue personalities will play any board game that has moving parts or lots of pieces. If we ask them what game they want to play, they may say, "Chutes and Ladders! The Game of Life! Wait, who wants to play outside? Who wants to go on a bike ride? Wait! What was the question?"

Blue personalities want action. Long, strategic, boring games won't satisfy their active personalities. They get distracted easily and the other players have to remind them when it is their turn. The blue personalities were too busy with other thoughts to pay attention to a slow game.

Red personalities? They want to play Monopoly. Actually, they want to dominate Monopoly. It is the best game ever! One winner. Get all the money. Control all the property. Rule with an iron fist.

Oh wait! There is Risk. In the game of Risk, we can conquer countries and conquer the world! What could possibly be better than that?

The green personalities? They will play by the rules - and they know every single rule. If there is even a small question about rules during the game, they will make sure to look it up in the rule book twice. The game must be played properly. What type of game do they like to play? Any game with math or facts or strategy.

Restaurant behavior.

Four children, four different personalities. We bring our four daughters to the restaurant. What happens?

The yellow personality? She makes sure everyone has their own menu, everyone has their glass of water filled. She is happy to recommend to the other children what they might like. And she will read the menu to her younger sisters while asking what they would like to eat.

The blue personality? She can't sit still. She wants to explore the restaurant. She has taken everyone's silverware and created a giant sculpture in the middle of the table. No one can read their menu because the blue personality wants to engage them in conversation.

Oh, and what should the blue personality eat? Well, she hasn't had time to look at the menu. But everything sounds like so much fun to try. When we ask her what she would like to eat, her reply is, "What are the different desserts I can eat when I am finished?"

The red personality? She wants to read her own menu. And yes, she knows exactly what she wants. No recommendations from other people, please. And when she has decided what she wants, she will gladly tell other people what they should eat. She wants to be an adult. She wants to be in charge. No children's meal for her. It must be the complete adult portion. She will give her order to the waiter directly, no help needed.

The green personality? Here is a chance to study the menu. What would be healthy? What would taste good? What looks familiar? The green personality may not want to try new and adventurous dishes. Familiar foods seem safer.

Finally, what about the parents? No matter what color personality the parents are, they will have to be patient. One set of instructions won't work for all four different color personality children.

Grandparents.

How do yellow personalities interact with their grandparents? They get everything they want.

How do blue personalities interact with their grandparents? They get everything they want.

How do red personalities interact with their grandparents? They get everything they want.

How do green personalities interact with their grandparents? They get everything they want.

So what is the problem here?

Grandparents.

Bedtime blues.

"Early to bed, early to rise." Sounds good. However, it doesn't work with children. For children, everything is brand-new. Life is a new learning experience. Why go to sleep when we could have so much more fun learning, participating, and just enjoying life?

That means going to bed is … terrible.

So how do the four color personalities act at bedtime? Again, we will exaggerate, but this helps us remember the different ways our children think.

The yellow personality? Bedtime would be easy if all our children were yellow personalities. They love to cooperate. They don't want to disappoint us. A simple story, told with love, is all they need. And a big hug and cuddle will do the trick.

Bedtime for yellow personalities gives them a chance to wind down from the day. With little prompting, they will brush their teeth, fold their clothes, put away their dirty laundry, and get ready for bed. Any happy story is fine with them.

The blue personality? Get ready for conflict. It is impossible for the blue personality to slow down and concentrate on being calm and relaxed. Too many thoughts in too many directions. So many things to do and experience. A chance to talk to more people. A chance to be active. Going to bed is pure torture for a blue personality.

Blue personalities have imagination. They will stall endlessly and create excuses for not going to bed. As parents, we will hear our blue personality children say:

- "I need a glass of water."
- "Please tell me another story."
- "I can't fall asleep. Let me go watch television."
- "I am bored. I cannot fall asleep. Let me get up."
- "There is something I forgot to do. I have to get out of bed now."
- "I need to get a book. I can't fall asleep now. I need to read."
- "My stomach hurts."
- "I'm hungry."
- "Can't I play another computer game?"
- "I don't want to go to sleep now. I am wide awake."
- "I can't go to sleep now. I am not tired."
- "Ask daddy to come and tell me another story."

The excuses are endless. Blue personality children hate going to bed.

As parents, our easiest solution is to let them be active until they collapse from exhaustion. Unfortunately, that may not happen until midnight.

No bedtime solution for the blue personality child has been discovered as of this date. Parents of blue personality children are doomed. We have to prepare ourselves for years of struggle.

The red personalities? Fortunately, they have more discipline. Because of their competitive nature, sometimes we can reason with them. We can assure them that going to bed on time will mean better performance the next day. They need to rest so that they can be #1 in their class, #1 in sports, #1 in everything.

Of course it is not always this easy. We might have to prepare for a long drawn-out argument about going to bed. Red personalities have strong wills. They want to be in total control of their schedules and their lives.

The green personalities? They are much less direct and seldom openly challenge our authority. They are easier to reason with. They enjoy the comfort of routines. That means a regular story every evening will make our job as parents easier.

Let's go shopping.

Yellow personalities enjoy the bonding time with their parents. Shopping is good quality time with them.

What do the yellow personalities do while shopping? They are thinking of their siblings. They are thinking of their friends. Shopping is not centered around what they want, but it means they can be looking for gifts for others.

What does shopping mean for blue personalities? A chance to run. A chance to explore. A chance to meet new people. Shopping is an adventure waiting to happen.

Keeping track of our blue personality children while shopping is an aerobic exercise. They want to experience life at its fullest, at hyperspeed. We might need caffeine before we take them shopping.

So what about the red personalities? They know exactly which stores they want to go to. And of course, they know exactly what they want. Let's prepare ourselves for a battle of wills when we take red personalities shopping.

It is easier to shop with green personalities. They tend not to wander. They enjoy the security of our company. However, getting them to make a decision might take some time. They want to make sure they have thought through all of the possibilities before making their final decision. We will have to be patient while they make up their minds.

Family reunions.

Family reunions are social. Yellow personalities enjoy these events. Here is a chance to catch up with cousins and other relatives.

These events also offer a chance to be helpful. The yellow personalities will enjoy helping to fix the food. Or, making the decorations could be fun also.

When playing with their relatives, the yellow personalities are keen to be team members. They won't be insisting that everyone plays their game or does their favorite activity.

Relationships and bonding are fun.

The blue personalities? Again, this is a chance to run, scream, be wild, and have fun. New people to meet. New activities. New ideas from their relatives. The blue personalities will be complaining, "Why do we have to go home now?"

Family reunions? Great fun!

Now, for the red personalities. Family reunions are a chance to show their leadership. They will suggest which activities everyone should do. If there are games, they will be the most competitive. They will want to organize their cousins into a big activity. Sure, some will think they are bossy, but to them, they are just leading the group.

While the green personalities are more introspective, they still will enjoy family reunions. For them, this is a chance to learn new things. Their relatives may have new ideas or new adventures that they can learn from. Green personalities don't have to be social to have fun.

And who talks the fastest?

The blue and red personalities are very direct, and will tend to talk faster. This is great when they interact with each other.

But who talks more slowly?

Usually the yellow and green personalities. They are less direct and tend to ponder things a bit longer. When they talk with each other, the conversations are paced and relaxed.

So we can see this coming, can't we?

When the fast talkers talk too fast, the slow talkers recoil and step back. And it is fun to watch the frustration on the fast talkers' faces when they have to patiently wait for the slow talkers to finish their sentences.

WHAT ARE THE WEAKNESSES OF THE FOUR COLOR PERSONALITIES?

All personalities have good characteristics and not-so-good characteristics. We don't want people to point out our weaknesses. However, knowing the possible challenges helps when we interact with our children. Here are some frustrations we can expect when dealing with the different color personalities.

- Yellow personalities? Sometimes they hate to leave their comfort zones. They feel better staying behind and feeling secure.

- Blue personalities? We can't expect them to remember everything. After all, they have 50 times more input with their hyperactive lives.

- Red personalities? Sometimes they forget about other people's feelings. This can bring some conflict and bad feelings.

- Green personalities? We wish they were more social and interacted with others more.

Weaknesses are like armpits. We all have them and they can sometimes stink.

Some weaknesses we can see right away, and adjust. Becoming a chameleon gives us a chance to adjust to our children's personalities.

Can we get our children to be more well-rounded and be color chameleons also? Sure we can. We just have to pace ourselves and not push too hard.

For example, our blue personality daughter, Ella, thought triathlon training sounded like fun. We quickly found out that 80% of triathletes (including their parents) are red personalities. Enough said. Ella loves team sports, so this was her first individual sport.

After several weeks of training, Ella's individual competitive spirit started to come out. Best of all, she was able to learn from the competitive reds and get along with them. What a great win-win, as she received an award for placing second in a triathlon a few months later. I bet her blue personality wore off on some of the competitive red personalities also.

But don't concentrate too much on the weaknesses. Instead, celebrate the great assets each personality brings. We want our children to grow up in a positive, supportive environment.

SHOULD WE TEACH THE COLOR PERSONALITIES TO OUR CHILDREN?

Yes! Children love to learn. They enjoy new clues to understanding their world.

When children learn about the color personalities, they have so much fun observing others.

- They can describe their friends better to their parents.
- They understand why Johnny acts like a bully on the playground.
- They learn how to get along with their teachers better.
- They learn how to cooperate with their friends.
- They know that Ella is going to dance, sing, jump and skip instead of quietly playing a board game.
- And they learn how to manipulate their parents better.

Huh? Yes, children learn quickly. They have to survive in a grown-up world. They don't have any money. They don't have any power.

So how will they survive? By looking for ways to negotiate and get what they want.

When they know that Mom is a red personality, and Dad is a yellow personality, who will they ask for cookies? It's obvious.

But when they have to be at practice on time, they will go directly to their red personality Mom to guarantee their on-time arrival.

Children adjust. They can learn their parents' color personalities and make things easier for everyone. So yes! Let's teach our children this wonderful skill.

We wish we had known about the color personalities when we were growing up. Don't you? Here is our chance to give our children a head-start on the world.

Worried that our children will use this color personality skill against us to get what they want? Of course. But, they are already pretty good at this. This skill will just make them a little more professional.

AS DADS, WE WANT OUR CHILD TO BE A BETTER VERSION OF US.

We love our children. We try to make their lives better. They should be healthier, smarter, and have more money than we did when we grew up. But sometimes we take it too far.

Soccer was my favorite sport in middle school. I endured the hot Texas sun to be the best I could be. The best part of my week? Practicing and playing soccer.

In first grade, my daughter wanted to try soccer. I went all in. I bought cleats for both of us, cones, a soccer ball and even spray-painted our back yard for practice drills and simulated games.

The team needed an assistant coach. I was the first to volunteer. My daughter and I were always the first to show up and the last to leave. The first season was a terrific bonding experience and I watched all the kids improve from day one.

After two seasons, she suddenly lost interest. Why? It doesn't matter. She just didn't want to play anymore. After confirming it was her personal decision, I was 100% okay with it. She wanted to try another sport.

Should she have stuck with soccer? Maybe, but she is a child. Why force her to do just one thing, and never experience any other options? She wanted to try volleyball, swim team, running, triathlons ... just to name a few. There is nothing worse than an overbearing parent, pushing his child to play a sport that doesn't interest his child. We can't relive our youth through our children.

I know my daughter, Ella, is a blue personality. She enjoys trying new sports and activities. Understanding her blue personality made it easier for me to "let go" and allow her to be herself.

WHY ISN'T THIS TAUGHT IN SCHOOL?

This subject wasn't covered in my grade school or high school years. My classes had 35+ students. There wasn't time for our teacher to work with over 35 different students during our short 45-minute classes. Hopefully, everyone in the class could be "average" and just fit in. Why? Because ...

- We get in trouble for not participating.
- We get in trouble for participating too much.
- We get in trouble for not speaking and just taking in the information.
- We get in trouble for talking too much and disrupting the class.
- We get in trouble for not showing enough creativity.
- We get in trouble for being the class clown.

Extreme opposites can lead to punishment. (Yes, I have experience. And yes, I caused all those situations.) No wonder we are taught to just fit in, just follow the rules, don't get in trouble, memorize stuff, and get good grades.

My favorite college course was "Human Motivation and Behavior." This course helped me understand that we are all different and that being unique is okay.

Let's help our children by letting them know that it is okay to be who they are.

Let's enjoy and celebrate the unique personalities of our children!

THANK YOU.

Thank you for purchasing and reading this book. I hope you found some ideas that will work for you.

Before you go, would it be okay if we asked a small favor? Would you take just one minute and leave a sentence or two reviewing this book on Amazon? Your review can help others choose what they will read next. It would be greatly appreciated by many fellow readers.

Get your FREE Four-Color
Personality Reference Sheet!

This one page sheet is a great way to quickly reference the colors and how to work with each. It is also an easy way to have your kids learn them too.

Download it now:

WhatsYourKidsColor.com

MORE FROM LIZ SCHREITER

How To Turn Your Mind Into A Fat-Burning Machine
15 Easy Ways To Lose The Weight and Never Find It Again.

Dieting is hard. Let your mind work for you, not against you.
Yes, you can manage your weight and still have a life!

Printed in Great Britain
by Amazon